JAPANESE COOKING
for
Kids

Recipes of
**Sumiko
Nagasawa**

Text by
**Kimberly
Ono**

ELTON-WOLF PUBLISHING

Japanese Cooking
for Kids

Cover art by Masami Shiga
Illustrations by Miho Sakai Moyer
Photography by Doug Wille
Japanese translation by Maria Wako
Hand modeling by Amy Tomaro and Bob Ono
Cover design by Jeanne Hendrickson
Text design by Sheila Hackler

Published by Elton-Wolf Publishing
Seattle, Washington

ISBN: 1-58619-049-0
Library of Congress Catalog Number: 2003107671
07 06 05 04 03   1 2 3 4 5

First Edition August 2003
Printed in South Korea

ELTON-WOLF PUBLISHING

2505 Second Avenue Suite 515 Seattle, Washington 98121
Tel 206.748.0345 Fax 206.748.0343
www.elton-wolf.com info@elton-wolf.com
Seattle • Los Angeles

Preface

Teaching a child to cook is educating at one of the most basic levels. In *Japanese Cooking For Kids,* we want to share food from Japan because it is at once healthy, beautiful, and interesting. Children preparing Japanese food will be learning to cook with natural ingredients; it is simply built into the cuisine.

Reading about holidays in this book, children of all ages will come to appreciate the beauty of Japanese culture and its rich traditions. Readers will sense how holiday celebrations go hand in hand with the food Japanese kids love to eat.

Japanese cooking, though unique in many ways and possibly new to you, is very accessible. Most of the dishes in this cookbook can be made with food that can be found at the local grocery store. For ingredients that you may not find there, such as **miso** (fermented soy bean) paste, there are oriental markets and health food shops that carry oriental foods.

It is helpful to know that the ingredients can be varied in many of these recipes. For example, **daikon** (Japanese radish) may be added to **nimono** (boiled vegetables), or the chicken in **ajigohan** (flavored rice) can be replaced by **asari** (small clams). Vegetables can be interchanged in **miso shiru** (soup made with miso) resulting in many delicious combinations. Feel free to experiment.

To further enhance the health benefits, more natural foods such as **genmai** (unpolished rice) or **haigamai** (rice with the germseed) and unrefined **kibisato** (millet sugar) may be used. Taste and nutrition are fine-tuned in Japanese cooking, each enhancing the other. It can truly be said that what you put into a dish, you will get back. We know you will enjoy introducing children to the world of Japanese cooking.

Contents

Introduction   xi

Japanese Ingredients   xiii

Guidelines for Shopping   xv

Measurements   xvi

Safety   xvi

Using Chopsticks   xvii

Oshougatsu—New Year's Day, January   1
  Apple Kinton: Japanese Sweet Potato and Apple   2

Mamemaki—Bean Throwing Ceremony, February   5
  Miso Shiru: Miso Soup   6

Hina Matsuri—Girl's Day, March   9
  Chirashizushi: Vinegared Rice with Colorful Toppings   10

Hanami—Flower Viewing, April   15
  Omusubi: Rice Balls   16

Kodomo no Hi—Children's Day, May   19
  Curry and Rice   20

Tsuyu—Rainy Season, June   23
  Ajisaikan: Hydrangea Flower Gelatin   24

Tanabata—Festival of the Weaver's Star, July   27
  Usuyakitamago: Japanese Omelet   28

Natsuyasumi—Summer Vacation, August   31
  Kakigouri: Shaved Ice   33

Otsukimikai—Harvest Moon Celebration, September   35
  Nimono: Boiled Vegetables   36

Tai'iku no Hi—Field Day, October   39
  Ajigohan: Flavored Rice   40

Imohori—Sweet Potato Digging, November   43
  Satsumaimo Youkan: Jellied Sweet Potato   44

Nenmatsu—End of the Year, December   47
  Toshikoshi Soba: Buckwheat Noodle Soup   50

Additional Recipes   53
  Tara Mushiyaki: Codfish Broiled in Foil   54
  Okayu: Rice Gruel   56
  Sumi's Sandwich House   59

Recipe Chart: Servings, Time, Difficulty   62

Recipes in Japanese   63

Glossary of Japanese Words and Phrases   85

Afterword to Parents and Teachers   89

Contributors   90

Introduction

"Hi, my name is Karen. I came to Japan with my family when I was six. I'm having a good time here. I go to an American school during the week, but Saturdays are different. I visit a Japanese lady. Her name is Sumiko Nagasawa. She's a cooking teacher, and she shows me how to make Japanese food. She also tells me stories about the ways people here celebrate holidays.

"When I first came to her apartment, I thought I was inside a dollhouse. It's so small! I take one step and I'm across the kitchen, another four and I've crossed the whole living-dining room. Dishes and teacups of every kind line the walls on shelves. She has handmade Japanese dishes as well as dishes from places like Brazil, France, and Switzerland. Believe it or not, there are three refrigerators–one for daily foods, one for foods with a strong odor, plus one to hold foods used in baking. And she has two ovens.

"I am just going to her place for a cooking lesson. Why don't you come along?"

"Hello, Sumi **Sensei** (teacher)."

"**Douzo ohairi kudasai** (please come in)."

"Thank you. I was just telling my new friends about you. I've been thinking about how much fun it is learning to make Japanese food. I bet children in other countries would enjoy cooking Japanese food too."

"Yes, I think so. We can show them how to make **chirashizushi and omusubi** and…"

"Don't go so fast! What's that in English?"

"**Chirashizushi** is rice with lots of colorful toppings and **omusubi** are rice balls. Got it?"

"Ok, I've got that. One thing I'm wondering, is whether kids can actually make Japanese food if they aren't living in Japan. They won't be shopping at Japanese grocery stores."

"There's no need to worry. I'm sure many stores sell Japanese foods nowadays. Also, I will tell how to substitute foods for ingredients that might not be available where they live."

"Well, great. Where do we start?"

"First we must take a look at some of these special ingredients."

Chirashizushi (chee-rah-shee-zoo-shee) – vinegared rice with colorful toppings
Douzo ohairi kudasai (dōh-zoh oh-hahee-ree koo-dah-sahee) – Please come in.
Omusubi (oh-moo-soo-bee) – rice balls. Also called **onigiri**.
Sensei (sen-sehee) – teacher

Japanese Ingredients

Ajinomoto (ah-jee-noh-moh-toh) – monosodium glutamate (MSG), a type of salt used for bringing out the flavor of foods. It may be omitted (It is not used in all-natural cooking).

Daikon (dahee-kon) – Japanese radish. You may substitute turnips.

Dashi (dah-shee) – soup stock made from dried fish. It is sold as loose flakes or shavings, in packets like tea bags or as a powder.

Enoki (eh-noh-kee) – nettle mushroom. You may substitute other mushrooms.

Gobo (goh-boh) – burdock root. You may omit.

Mirin (mee-reen) – sweetened Japanese rice wine, used only for cooking. You may omit.

Miso (mee-soh) – fermented soy bean paste

Negi (neh-gee) – long onion. You may substitute leeks.

Niban dashi (nee-ban dah-shee) – second broth, made from once-boiled dried fish used for **dashi.**

Nori (noh-ree) – laver, a seaweed that is pressed into sheets and dried.

Sake (sah-keh) – rice wine. You may substitute cooking sherry.

Ajinomoto

Daikon

Dashi

Enoki

Gobo

Dashi

Rice Vinegar

Mirin

Sake

Miso

Negi

Nori

Japanese Ingredients (continued)

Satoimo (sah-toh-ee-moh) – taro, plant similar to a potato. You may substitute white potatoes.

Satsumaimo (sah-tsoo-mahee-moh) – Japanese sweet potato. You may substitute yams.

Shiitake (shee ee-tah-keh) – large flat mushroom. You may use fresh or dried. You may substitute other mushrooms.

Soba (soh-bah) – buckwheat or buckwheat noodles. You may substitute instant ramen.

Takenoko (tah-keh-noh-koh) – bamboo shoot. You may substitute water chestnuts.

Tara (tah-rah) – codfish. You may substitute other white fish such as tilapia, orange roughy or halibut.

Tofu (toh-foo) – soybean curd

Ume boshi (oo-meh boh-shee) – pickled plum

Wakame (wah-kah-meh) – variety of seaweed, usually dried or partially dried. You may substitute spinach.

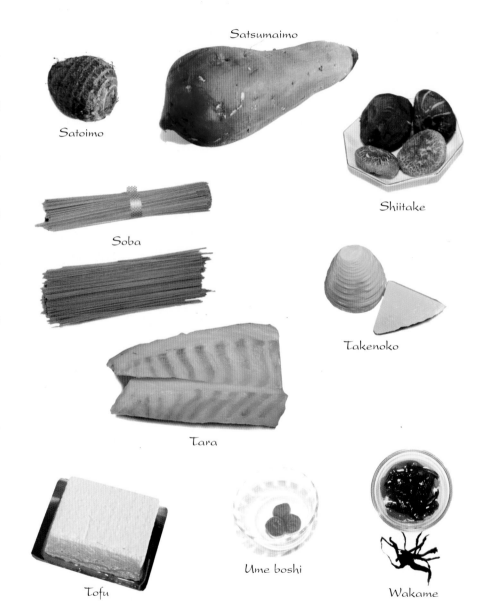

Satsumaimo

Satoimo

Shiitake

Soba

Takenoko

Tara

Tofu

Ume boshi

Wakame

Guidelines for Shopping

Sumi **Sensei** teaches that it is important to buy healthy food such as fresh vegetables, good meat, and natural food without preservatives. If you can't find the authentic Japanese ingredients, go ahead and substitute using the food listed, or be creative and try one of your own substitutions.

Rice is different in different countries. The type that is most like Japanese rice is high gluten rice. It is sticky like the rice in Japan. If possible use this type or use medium grain rice. Also, rice is cooked differently from place to place. For example, in Japan it is always rinsed several times before using. In America, however, rice is usually not rinsed. In fact, instructions on the bag often say not to rinse it. We have found that this rice holds its shape better if it is wet once with water and allowed to stand in a colander 15–30 minutes before cooking.

Sensei (sen-sehee) – teacher

Measurements

◆ One cup is the American standard, equal to 225 ml.

◆ One tablespoon is equal to 15 ml.

◆ Vegetables are standard American sizes; for example, skinny carrots and fat cucumbers.

Safety

Be sure to observe the basic guidelines for safety in the kitchen. First, wash your hands before you begin. Handle sharp knives properly. For fire safety, never leave the kitchen when something is cooking on the stove. Ask someone to watch the stove if you must leave the area. When steaming food, avoid reaching into the pan while it is still hot. Remove the pan from the heat then carefully remove the lid. After most of the steam has escaped, carefully take out the food.

◆ Small children should have an adult with them at all times when they cook. ◆

Using Chopsticks

In Japan, people use chopsticks to eat their food. There are short chopsticks for children, and they start using them around age five. To use them, place the bottom chopstick against the tip of your fourth finger running across to the wedge by your thumb and pointer finger. Place the top chopstick between your second and third finger and steady it with the tip of your thumb. Move the top one up and down and let the bottom one stay still.

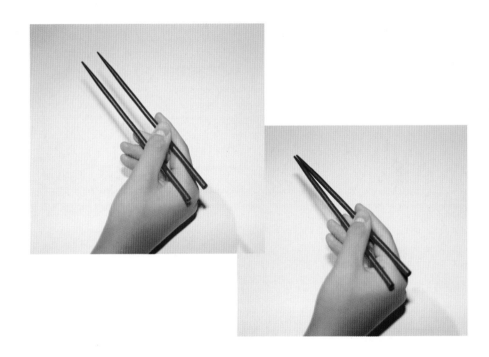

Akemashite omedetou gozaimasu (ah-keh-mah-shee-teh oh-meh-deh-tōh goh-zahee-mah-soo) – Happy New Year

Kinton (keen-ton) – sweet dish made with sweet potatoes and boiled chestnuts or apples

Osechiryouri (oh-seh-chee-reeyōh-ree) – Japanese traditional food often prepared with a lot of salt or sugar as preservatives

Otoshidama (oh-toh-shee-dah-mah) – money given to children at New Year's

Sensei (sen-sehee) – teacher

Oshougatsu

New Year's Day
January 1

"**Akemashite omedetou gozaimasu.** I wish you a very happy New Year, Karen. Now let's get started with our cooking lesson. Did you understand what I told you about practicing safety in the kitchen?"

"Yes. When I cook at home my older sister helps me. It works out fine. Sumi **Sensei**, tell me about the traditional New Year's Day in Japan."

"This is the biggest holiday in Japan. There's no school, and almost everyone is off from work on January 1st, 2nd, and 3rd. Children visit their grandparent's home where they see lots of colorful food arranged in lacquer boxes. This is called **osechiryouri**, and they eat it for breakfast, lunch, and supper during the entire holiday. When guests pay a visit, they are also served some of these very sweet or salty dishes. Children are glad when visitors arrive because they usually bring a little envelope with money inside called **otoshidama**.

"One of the dishes served is **kinton** (sweet potato and chestnuts). Traditionally it is made very, very sweet so that it won't spoil. I like to make it with crunchy apples instead of chestnuts. I call it Apple **Kinton**."

Apple Kinton

Japanese Sweet Potato and Apple

What You Need

2-3 **satsumaimo** (a little over 1 lb)
(Yams may be substituted)

3 tablespoons sugar

1 medium apple

lemon juice

dash of salt (optional)

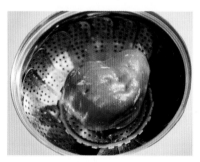

1. Steam the satsumaimo

What to Do

1. Steam or boil the **satsumaimo** until they are very soft when pierced with a fork (30–40 minutes). Or microwave for about 10 minutes.

2. Remove from pan or microwave and let cool a bit. Peel off the skin with your fingers. Discard it.

3. Mash the **satsumaimo** using a fork or potato masher. This is fun. A food processor will do the job also.

4. Stir in the sugar.

5. Wash, peel and dice the apple. (If no chemical pesticides were used, the peel can be left on.) Soak in a bowl of water with a few drops of lemon juice so the apple won't turn brown.

6. Drain the diced apple and mix into the **satsumaimo**. Check the taste. Add more sugar if you want it sweeter. Add a dash of salt if you like.

2. Peel off the skin

3. Mash

Serve on small plates. This is a great dessert or after-school snack.

Before eating say, "**Itadakimasu** (I take this to eat)."

After eating say, "**Gochisousamadeshita** (I enjoyed this food or drink very much)."

6. Mix

Fuku wa uchi! Oni wa soto! (foo-koo wah oo-chee oh-nee wah soh-toh) – Blessings come into the house and devil get out!

Miso shiru (mee-soh shee-roo) – soup made with miso

Sensei (sen-sehee) – teacher

Setsubun (seh-tsoo-boon) – roughly translated: Spring is just around the corner.

Mamemaki

Bean Throwing Ceremony
February 3

"Fuku wa uchi! Oni wa soto!"

"Why are you shouting, Sumi **Sensei?**"

"I'm asking blessings and fortune to come into my home and telling the devil to get out. On February 3rd everybody—children, parents, and grandparents—shouts these words while throwing roasted beans around the house. White beans, for good fortune, are tossed inside, and black ones, representing evil, are thrown outside into the garden. I live in an apartment, so I have to be satisfied throwing the black beans out onto my balcony. The third is also the day to celebrate **Setsubun,** which means 'Spring is just around the corner.'"

"What recipe shall we prepare this month, **Sensei?**"

"It's cold in February, so how about a warm bowl of **miso shiru** (fermented soy bean paste soup)?"

"OK. Sounds good. I like soup."

Miso Shiru

Miso Soup

What You Need

4 cups water

3 heaping tablespoons **dashi** flakes
    (or 1 packet **dashi** flakes,
    or 1 tablespoon powdered **dashi**)

Choice of vegetable combinations:
    3/4 cup potato
    3 tablespoons **wakame** (or spinach)

    1 block **tofu** (3 inch x 3 inch)
    3 tablespoons spinach

    3/4 to 1 cup **daikon** (or turnip)
    1/4 cup **negi** (or onion)

3 tablespoons **miso** paste

What to Do

1. Bring the water to a boil. Add the **dashi**. Turn off heat and let sit for about 5 minutes. This makes the soup stock.

2. Remove **dashi** packet or strain the soup stock into another pan if using **dashi** flakes.*

3. Chop potato into bite-size pieces. Add it to the stock and simmer until tender.

4. Prepare the **wakame** by rinsing the salt off. Soak it in some water while the potato is cooking. Rinse again and chop into bite-size pieces. Put some into each soup bowl. Set aside.

5. Add the **miso** paste to the soup a little at a time. Get two tablespoons. Hold a spoon full of paste in one hand. Lower it halfway into the soup then rub the paste off the spoon and into the soup with the spoon held in the other hand. (It's not as hard as it sounds.) Heat through.

6. Ladle the soup into the bowls with the **wakame**.

1. Add the dashi.

2. Strain the stock.

3. Chop the potato.

5. Add the miso paste.

To make soup with **tofu** and spinach, first drain the liquid off the **tofu**. Rinse off the spinach and chop into bite-size pieces. Add these last, after the **miso** has been stirred in. (If overcooked, **tofu** breaks up easily and spinach loses its bright green color.)

For the **daikon** and **negi** version, chop the **daikon** and simmer it in the soup stock. Add finely chopped **negi** during the last couple of minutes of cooking. Stir in the **miso**.

* In Japanese cooking, there is little waste. Sumi **Sensei** makes **niban dashi** out of the once-boiled flakes. Simmer flakes in 1/2 the amount of water first used. Strain. Use in preparing other dishes.

Chirashizushi (chee-rah-shee-zoo-shee) – vinegared rice with colorful toppings

Hinadan (hee-nah-dan) – Girl's Day decoration consisting of miniature pieces representing a royal court

Ohimesama (oh-hee-meh-sah-mah) – princess

Ouji (ōh-jee) – prince

Hina Matsuri

Girl's Day
March 3

"Karen, come in. I have something special to show you. This is the decoration for Girl's Day. It's called a **hinadan**. All the miniature pieces represent a royal court. See the fancy box on the bottom step. It might hold food or other items. Ladies-in-waiting are on the next step. **Ohimesama** (princess) and **ouji** (prince) are on the top step."

"It's fantastic! Did you have a **hinadan** like this when you were growing up?"

"Oh yes, but the one in my home was larger. It had seven steps and actually took up one whole corner of the room. I could sit and gaze at it for hours. My mother made special snacks for Girl's Day, and we had a little tea party together every afternoon after school. The celebration went on for about a week. It was wonderful. I've prepared one of these snacks for us to have today. It's called **chirashizushi** (vinegared rice with colorful toppings). I will teach you and your friends to make it too."

"What fun—a Japanese tea party!"

Chirashizushi

Vinegared Rice with Colorful Toppings

What You Need

2 cups uncooked rice

2 1/4 cups water

Vinegar Mixture:

    1/3 cup vinegar

    2 tablespoons sugar

    1 1/2 teaspoons salt

    2 tablespoons sesame seeds

      (optional)

What to Do

1. Rinse the rice in a big bowl. Use your hands, it's fun! Drain off the cloudy water after rinsing. Repeat this step 3 or 4 times, then put rice into a colander, cover, and let it stand 15–30 minutes.

Note: The instructions on some bags of rice say not to rinse it. If so, put the rice in a colander, wet with water, cover, and let stand 15–30 minutes

1b. Let it stand

2. Choose a heavy pot that is much deeper than the amount of raw rice. Put the rice in and add the water. Cover.

3. Bring to a boil over medium-high heat. Lower the heat and let the rice boil gently for about 10–12 minutes until all the water is absorbed.

1. Rinse the rice

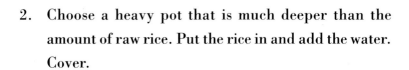

2. Add water

4. Turn off heat and let stand covered, for 5–6 minutes.

5. Put it into a big bowl (wooden if you have one).

6. Mix vinegar, sugar, and salt together, then pour over the rice. Gently fluff rice with a wooden spatula. Fan the rice while doing this, for quick cooling. Keep fanning until the rice no longer lets off steam. This is when another pair of hands is welcome. Mix in sesame seeds now. Set aside.

6. Pour vinegar mixture over rice

6b. Fluff rice while fanning

Continued

Chirashizushi

Vinegared Rice with Colorful Toppings

Continued

Toppings:

5 **shiitake**

   (or Chinese black mushroom)

   1 tablespoon soy sauce

   1 tablespoon sugar

   1 tablespoon **mirin** (optional)

2 eggs

3/4 cup frozen mixed vegetables

1 3 1/2-ounce can of crabmeat

3 slices of boiled sandwich ham

1/2 cucumber, unpeeled

1 sheet **nori** (optional)

7. If using dried **shiitake**, soak them in a little hot water until soft. Squeeze the excess water out. Cut off the stems, discard. Slice the caps into thin strips. If you are using fresh **shiitake**, just cut off the stems and slice the caps. Put sliced **shiitake** in a small pan. Add just enough water to cover them. Add the soy sauce, sugar and **mirin**. Simmer over low heat about 5 minutes or until most of the water is gone. Watch the pan carefully, soy sauce and sugar will burn after the water is gone. Remove **shiitake** from pan and set aside.

7. Slice shiitake

8. In a frying pan with some oil, scramble the eggs, adding a pinch of salt.

Note: Traditionally **usuyakitamago**, a very thin omelet, cut into strips, is used. See page 29.

9. To defrost the mixed vegetables, place them in a colander and pour boiling water over them. Pat dry with a paper towel.

10. Drain the crabmeat.

11. Wash the cucumber and slice it into long, thin strips, then cut the strips into pieces about 1 inch long. Slice the ham the same way.

12. Lightly mix these into the rice. Save half of the eggs and ham.

13. **Chirasu** (sprinkle) the remaining half of the eggs and ham on top. Use scissors to cut the **nori** into thin strips and sprinkle on top of everything.

12. Lightly mix

To serve, place in the center of the table and give everyone a small plate. Everyone helps themselves. A bowl of chicken bouillon soup makes a great side dish.

Obento (oh-ben-toh) – Japanese box lunch

Omusubi (oh-moo-soo-bee) – rice balls. Also called **onigiri.**

Sakura (sah-koo-rah) – cherry tree or blossom

Sensei (sen-sehee) – teacher

Hanami

Flower Viewing
April

"Sumi **Sensei**, what's your favorite season?"

"There's nothing like cherry blossom time in Japan. Can you imagine big strong trees with thousands of delicate pale pink blossoms? From a distance these trees look like they are wrapped in light pink clouds.

"We Japanese want to be outside–right under the **sakura** (cherry trees). It's time to go on a picnic. Families, friends, or groups of people from work pack box lunches (or suppers) called **obento.** They go to a park and find a good spot under a beautiful cherry tree. Then they eat, drink, talk, and sing songs for hours. The main items in these lunch boxes are **omusubi** (rice balls). I'll show you how to make them."

Omusubi

What You Need

1 cup rice

1 1/4 cups water

small bowl with water

1 teaspoon salt

Optional fillings:
  canned tuna, drained
  boiled sandwich ham,
    cut into bite-size pieces
  cooked chicken,
    cut into bite-size pieces
  cooked salmon, flaked

nori

Rice Balls

What to Do

1. Cook the rice as described on page 10.

2. Let it cool down a bit so it will be easier to handle.

3. Add salt to the bowl of water and stir to dissolve. The water should taste slightly salty.

4. Dip your hands into the salt water to wet them. Divide the rice into 4–5 balls.

4. Divide into 4–5 balls

5. Dip again and shake off any rice still stuck to your hands. Now take a ball and press it firmly into the palm of one hand. Turn the ball, press, then repeat: turn, press, turn, press. (Dip your hand into the salt water if rice starts to stick.) It's like making a snowball. The goal is to make a rice ball that holds together but is not packed so tightly that the rice is smashed or broken down.

"This is not easy," says Sumi **Sensei**. "**Gambate ne** (hang in there)!"

5. Press firmly

5b. Gently poke a hole

You can add things like tuna, chicken, or ham to the middle of the rice balls while shaping them. Sumi **Sensei** prefers tuna. Gently poke a hole into the rice ball. Put a small amount of filling into the hole, pushing it down to the center. Press some rice over the hole to cover it.

6.   Now wrap a piece of **nori** on the outside of the rice ball.

Eat this snack now or wrap in plastic and have later. No chopsticks needed. A rice ball is definitely finger food.

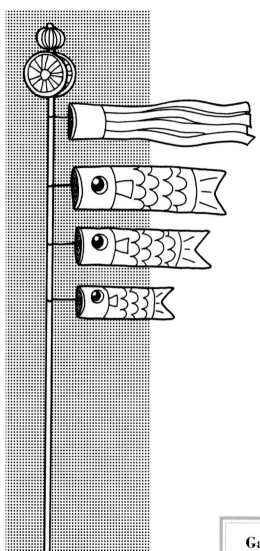

Gambate ne! (gam-bah-teh neh) – Hang in there!

Koinobori (kohee-noh-boh-ree) – carp streamer or windsock. It looks like a kite.

Samurai (sah-moo-rahee) – a Japanese warrior

Sensei (sen-sehee) – teacher

Kodomo no Hi

Children's Day
May 5

"Sumi **Sensei,** what is Children's Day? I remember we had Girl's Day in March. Don't the boys have a Boy's Day?"

"Well, Karen, for a long time May 5th was Boy's Day in celebration of the boys in a family. Now it is a national holiday celebrating both boys and girls. There are special decorations just as there are for Girl's Day. A doll-like figure of a boy dressed up as a **samurai** (warrior) is often displayed in the home to honor boys. Outside, something like giant windsocks in the shape of fish with their mouths wide open can be seen flapping in the breeze. These flying carp are called **koinobori**, and when the wind blows they appear to be struggling to swim upstream."

"I guess that is supposed to mean something."

"Of course. Boys and girls have to try hard to overcome difficulty at times. We have a saying in Japanese for this. **Gambate ne!** You say, 'Hang in there.' For our recipe this month how about some curry and rice to strengthen you for the task?"

"Sounds good to me. Just thinking about overcoming all those obstacles has made me hungry!"

Curry and Rice

What You Need

2 cups rice

2 1/4 cups water

Curry Sauce *

    2/3 cup milk

    2 1/2–3 tablespoons curry powder

    3 tablespoons flour

1 pound meat (beef or chicken)

salt and pepper

3 potatoes

4 carrots

1 onion

2 tablespoons vegetable oil

1 1/2 cups water

1 1/2 cubes beef or chicken bouillon

1 teaspoon salt

1 medium apple

What To Do

1. Cook the rice as described on page 10.

2. To make the curry sauce, heat milk in a small pan over low heat. Add the curry powder and flour a little at a time while stirring. The mixture will be quite thick. Turn off heat. Set aside.

3. Now cut the meat into large bite-size pieces.

4. Peel the carrots and chop them into bite-size pieces.

5. Wash and peel the potatoes then chop into bite-size chunks. Put them into a bowl of water so that they won't turn brown.

6. Peel the onion and cut into pieces the same size as the other vegetables.

7. In a heavy pot, over medium heat, heat the oil. Cook the meat and vegetables until the meat is brown and the onions are soft. (Be sure to drain the potatoes before adding them to the pot.) Add a little salt and pepper.

8. Now add the bouillon, salt and water. Stir well.

2. Make the curry sauce

6. Cut onion

10. Stir in curry sauce

9. Cover and simmer over medium heat until the meat is cooked through; about 10 minutes.

10. Add the curry sauce, which is more like a paste. Stir it in a little at a time. * Instant curry mix may be used. Follow instructions on the package.

11. Peel the apple and grate it. Add it to the pot. Mix well.

12. Cover and simmer all ingredients over low heat about 40 minutes so the flavors can blend. Stir every once in awhile so the food won't stick to the bottom of the pot. Taste and add more salt if needed.

11. Grate apple

To serve, put some rice in a bowl then spoon the curry mixture next to it. Decorate with a sprig of parsley if you like. A green salad completes the meal nicely.

Ajisai (ah-jee-sahee) – hydrangea flower
Sensei (sen-sehee) – teacher

Tsuyu

Rainy Season
June

"**Sensei**, it sure is cloudy a lot these days."

"You're right. This is the month to expect rain and more rain. In the southern areas of Japan it rains almost every day. I had to get used to that when I was growing up. Even though the days are cloudy and gray, you can still see lots of color outside. Big blue or pink hydrangea flowers called **ajisai** are in bloom, and people like to carry colorful umbrellas."

"I just get so bored when it's raining. I can't think of enough to do."

"Is that so? Well, why don't you try something really creative like making an edible hydrangea flower?"

"You must be kidding!"

"Of course not. Read on!"

Ajisaikan

Hydrangea Flower Gelatin

What You Need

2 1/2 cups water

2 1/2 tablespoons gelatin
(three 1 oz packages)

4 tablespoons sugar

2 tablespoons grape juice concentrate
(frozen is OK)

1/4 teaspoon peppermint extract

5 tablespoons milk

several leaves from **ajisai** (hydrangea)
or other green plant for
decoration.

Avoid a plant that has just been
sprayed. It could make you sick.

What to Do

1. Heat water in a pan. Turn off heat.

2. Sprinkle the gelatin over the water. Let stand for 3 minutes.

3. Turn heat back on low. Add sugar and stir until dissolved.

4. Pour the liquid into 4 different containers. Choose ones
    with flat bottoms if possible. Try to divide the liquid
    equally between them.

*2. Sprinkle gelatin
over water*

5. Add the grape juice concentrate to one of the containers. Stir.

6. Add peppermint extract to another container. Stir.

7. Add milk to the third container and stir.

8. Put a lid on the containers or cover lightly with plastic wrap. Refrigerate the 3
    containers with flavoring until gelatin is firm, about 1 hour.

9. Wait 30 minutes then refrigerate the container of unflavored gelatin about 30
    minutes for a soft set.

10. Select a clear serving bowl about 6 in. (15 cm) wide. Wet the inside with water.

11. Remove the 3 containers of flavored gelatin from the refrigerator. Cut the gelatin
    into different shapes – squares, circles, stars, etc. Each piece should be about
    1/2 inch across. Gently place them in the serving bowl. Mix the colors as you go.

If the gelatin sticks to the container and you can't get it out, set it in a pan of hot water for
about 15 seconds. This will melt the bottom portion of the gelatin, and it will slide out easily.

4. Pour into 4 containers

7. Add the milk and stir

11. Place gelatin pieces in bowl

12. Wash the green leaves and place them around the edge of the gelatin, sticking partway under. The tips of the leaves should stick out of the bowl a bit. You are creating a big flower in a bowl.

13. Remove the container of unflavored gelatin from the refrigerator. It should be soft but not runny. Spoon it over the top of the flavored gelatin. This will be a sort of glaze finish for this creation. Refrigerate again for about 15 minutes.

To serve, place the hydrangea flower in the center of the table. Spoon out small portions of the gelatin into individual bowls. The leaves are not to eat! This is a great dessert or snack. Add tea and a cookie, and it's just right.

Chirashizushi (chee-rah-shee-zoo-shee) – vinegared rice with colorful toppings

Origami (oh-ree-gah-mee) – folded paper figures

Orihime (oh-ree-hee-meh) – Weaver or Vega star

Tanabata (tah-nah-bah-tah) – Festival of the Weaver's star

Sensei (sen-sehee) – teacher

Ushiboshi (oo-shee-boh-shee) – Cowherd or Altair star

Usuyakitamago (oo-soo-yah-kee-tah-mah-goh) – thin rolled omelet

Tanabata

Festival of the Weaver's Star
July 7

"**Sensei**, I can't believe Japanese kids have to go to school until the end of July!"

"Well, that's how it is here. While dreaming of the upcoming summer vacation, children look up into the night sky and remember the love story of two stars. **Orihime** (Weaver or Vega star) and **Ushiboshi** (Cowherd or Altair star) only get to meet one night of the year. That night is the seventh night of the seventh month–**Tanabata**. In Japan we celebrate this day by decorating large arching bamboo shoots with colorful **origami** (folded paper figures). They are hung on the bamboo, sort of like ornaments on a Christmas tree."

"Is there a special dish for **Tanabata**?"

"We Japanese like to eat **chirashizushi** (vinegared rice with colorful toppings) with carrots cut into the shape of stars."

"We already made that."

"You are right. We made it with scrambled eggs, but now I'll show you how to make the more delicate **usuyakitamago** (thin rolled omelet)."

Usuyakitamago   Japanese Omelet

What You Need

frying pan, 6 inch (15 cm)

vegetable oil

3 eggs

1 teaspoon sugar

1 teaspoon soy sauce

mayonnaise

thin slices of cucumber, unpeeled

What to Do

1. Mix

1. In a small bowl, mix eggs, sugar, and soy sauce well.

2. Grease the frying pan with oil. (If the oil pools, there's too much. Carefully remove some with a paper towel.)

3. Place the pan over low heat.

4. Pour in 1/3 of the egg mixture. Pick up the pan and tip it to spread the mixture evenly. Cook until the egg mixture hardens, about 1 minute. Remove the pan from heat.

5. Using a spatula, loosen the omelet from the far edge of the pan. Roll omelet toward you.

5. Roll omelet toward you

6. Remove the rolled omelet from the pan and place it on a chopping board. Unroll the omelet.

7. Using a paper towel spread a little more oil on the pan.

8. Return the pan to the heat and pour in 1/2 the remaining egg mixture.

9. Cook as before, remove, and place on top of the first omelet.

10. Repeat with the last bit of egg mixture.

11. Roll up the stacked omelets. Make a tight roll. Slice into 1 1/2 inch lengths.

11. Make a tight roll

As you improve you will be able to make thinner omelets by pouring in less egg mixture each time.

To serve, place on a small plate with the cut side up. Spoon a little mayonnaise on top. Don't spread it. Now place some cucumber slices on the mayonnaise. In Japan, **usuyakitamago** is eaten cold.

Juku (joo-koo) – cram school

Kakigouri (kah-kee-gōh-ree) – shaved ice with flavored syrup

Kanji (kan-jee) – Chinese characters

Sensei (sen-sehee) – teacher

Natsuyasumi

Summer Vacation
August

"Hi, Karen, come in. It's very hot today, isn't it?"

"No kidding. It's so muggy, too. I wish I was going to America for vacation this year. I wonder what I am going to do this whole month!"

"Well, here the best thing to do is get into the water. You could go to the city pool with friends to enjoy fancy slides, wave action, and even a pool with a current to push you along. It's great. Many families take a short trip to the seaside where they can experience some real wave action. Do you think Japanese kids are free to play every day, though?"

"I hope so! If I only had five weeks for summer vacation, I'd go to the pool every day."

"No way. There's summer homework to be done. There are math problems, writing **kanji** (Chinese characters), a special science project, as well as the daily diary entry. Quite a few children even go to **juku** (cram school) a few hours a day for even more study. What do you think about this?"

"I'll pass on the homework and going to cram school, but I'll definitely go to the pool. Since I'm here, let's make something. What is a good treat to make in summer?"

"Ice is the coldest thing you can eat, right? Japanese kids love **kakigouri** (shaved ice) with syrup. Let's make some."

Use a spoon to eat this treat. (It should not be slushy enough to drink through a straw.)

Kakigouri

Shaved Ice

What You Need

ice shaver or food processor

2 cups of ice cubes per person

3 tablespoons fruit syrup

Some choices:
> strawberry
> blueberry
> grape
> melon
> lime

What to Do

1. Put the ice into the ice shaver or food processor.

2. Grind it into fine shavings.

3. Put into a bowl or large cup.

4. Carefully pour the fruit syrup on top.

1. Put ice into ice shaver

2. Grind into fine shavings

4. Pour fruit syrup on top

Nimono (nee-moh-noh) – boiled vegetables

Obento (oh-ben-toh) – Japanese box lunch

Roujin no Hi (rōh-jeen noh hee) – Respect for the Elderly Day

Sensei (sen-sehee) – teacher

Shuubun (shoo-boon) – day and night are equal but days will start to get shorter

Susuki (soo-soo-kee) – Japanese pampas grass

Otsukimikai

Harvest Moon Celebration
September

"Hi, Karen. Did you start back to school this week?"

"Yes, I started on Wednesday."

"Do you know one big difference between Japanese and American school systems?"

"I heard that all students have to wear white shoes inside the school building."

"Besides that! April is when the school year starts and kids move up a grade, not September. There are two national holidays in September. **Roujin no Hi** (Respect for the Elderly) and **Shuubun** (when day and night are an equal number of hours). After this the days will become shorter. The harvest of crops begins.

"It's the last chance for an evening picnic. I like to spread out a mat facing the harvest moon, full and low in the sky. Crickets sing and **susuki** (Japanese pampas grass) shines in the moonlight. I always include **nimono** (boiled vegetables) in my **obento**. I'll teach you how to make them."

"Hmmm, Sumi **Sensei**, vegetables? Do you know how most kids feel about eating vegetables!"

Nimono

Boiled Vegetables

What You Need

3 **shiitake** (or other mushroom)

2 carrots

3 medium size **satoimo**
(or 2 white potatoes)

10–12 snow peas

4 ounces dark chicken meat

3 tablespoons **takenoko**
(or water chestnuts)

1 1/2 cups **niban dashi** (see page 7)
(You may use regular **dashi.**)

1 tablespoon sugar

2 tablespoons soy sauce

2 tablespoons **sake**
(or cooking sherry)

2 tablespoons **mirin** (optional)

pinch **ajinomoto** (optional)

What to Do

1. If using dried **shiitake**, soak in a little hot water until soft.

2. Peel carrot and cut into large bite-size pieces.

3. Wash the **satoimo** and peel. Be careful, these can be slippery. Soak in cold water.

4. Wash the snow peas, remove head and string and set aside.

5. Cut chicken into small bite-size pieces.

6. If using fresh **takenoko**, rinse it off and slice into bite-size pieces. If using canned, drain the liquid off.

7. Drain the **shiitake** and **satoimo**. Save the liquid from the **shiitake**. Cut the stem off the **shiitake**. Leave the **satoimo** whole or cut it in half if it is large.

8. Place all the vegetables and chicken into a pan. Do not add the snow peas. Add the **niban dashi**, sugar, soy sauce and **sake**. Add the liquid from the dried **shiitake**. Bring to a boil then lower the heat. Simmer until vegetables are tender, about 12 minutes.

4. Remove head and string from snow peas

8. Add the dashi

9. Add snow peas last

9. Add the **mirin** the last few minutes of cooking, along with the snowpeas. Add a pinch of **ajinomoto** to enhance the flavor if desired. Stir well.

To serve, spoon into a bowl along with some remaining juices from the pan. In Japan vegetables are eaten either hot or at room temperature.

Aikido (ahee-kee-doh) – a Japanese martial art

Ajigohan (ah-jee-goh-han) – flavored rice

Kendo (ken-doh) – Japanese fencing

Obento (oh-ben-toh) – Japanese box lunch

Sensei (sen-sehee) – teacher

Undokai (oon-doh-kahee) – athletic meet

Tai'iku no Hi

Field Day
October 10

"**Sensei,** is it true October 10th is a national holiday?"

"That's right. On this day sounds of cheering, laughter, and of course peppy marching band-style music fill the air around schools. It's the day of **undokai** (athletic meet) when students participate in favorite outdoor games like tug-of-war, spoon races, relay races, and beanbag tosses. Some schools also feature traditional Japanese games such as **aikido** (a martial art) and **kendo** (Japanese fencing). This is a family day. Parents come to watch, and they even participate in the games."

"Let me guess. Everybody takes an **obento** for lunch."

"Of course. Now, what else can I teach the kids to make for a box lunch? I know. **Ajigohan** (flavored rice), will be just right."

"Another rice dish? I am surprised there are so many ways to cook rice!"

Ajigohan

Flavored Rice

What You Need

2 cups rice

2 1/2 cups liquid, total

1 chicken breast (about 6 oz)

1 1/2 tablespoons soy sauce

1 1/2 tablespoons **sake**
    (or cooking sherry)

1 tablespoon sugar

1/2 carrot

5 inches **gobo** root (optional)

3 tablespoons **enoki** tops
    (or other mushroom)

3 tablespoons **takenoko**
    (or water chestnut)

1 tablespoon soy sauce

2 tablespoons parsley

What to Do

1. Wash the rice as described on page 10.

2. Cut the chicken into small pieces.

3. Put it into a pan and add just enough water to cover. Add 1 1/2 tablespoons soy sauce, **sake** and sugar.

4. Boil until the meat is cooked through, about 5 minutes.

5. Remove chicken. Save the liquid.

6. Peel the carrot and cut into thin slices 1/2 inch long.

7. Peel the **gobo** root with a potato peeler. Cut it into very thin slices. Soak in a bowl of water to prevent it from turning brown. (**Gobo** root oxidizes very fast.)

8. If using fresh **takenoko,** rinse it off and slice into small pieces. For canned, drain off the liquid.

3. Add soy sauce

7. Cut gobo

9. Add water to make 2 1/2 cups

9. Put vegetables and chicken into a pot. Add just enough water to the liquid left from boiling the chicken to make 2 1/2 cups. Add 1 tablespoon soy sauce and a pinch of salt. Add liquid to pot. Stir.

10. Cook over low heat about 12 minutes, taking care not to burn the rice.

11. Let the rice stand for 15 minutes. Fluff it with a fork, then gently stir in the minced parsley.

9b. Stir

Use this for a box lunch or serve at home along with some egg-drop soup and mandarin orange slices for dessert.

Satsumaimo (sah-tsoo-mahee-moh) – Japanese sweet potato

Satsumaimo youkan (sah-tsoo-mahee-moh yōh-kan) – jellied sweet potato

Imohori

Sweet Potato Digging
November

"Karen, have you noticed that during autumn in Japan you often see little children wearing rain boots on a perfectly clear day?"

"Why is that?"

"They are going sweet potato digging and will be up to their knees in dirt. After a short half hour of digging with a little shovel, lots and lots of oblong reddish-brown potatoes will have been harvested These sweet potatoes, or **satsumaimo**, taste great roasted outside in a pile of raked leaves. I enjoyed doing this as a child."

" Besides roasting them, is there anything else you can do with sweet potatoes? "

"Oh, there are quite a few recipes to make with **satsumaimo**. I'll teach you how to make a very traditional Japanese snack. It's called **satsumaimo youkan** (jellied sweet potato)."

"What if Japanese sweet potatoes aren't available?"

"I believe you have a sweet potato in America called a yam. Yams have a stronger taste than **satsumaimo** and are a darker color inside, but their texture is almost the same. You can use them to make this snack."

Satsumaimo Youkan   Jellied Sweet Potato

What You Need

2–3 **satsumaimo** (a little over 1 lb)
(Yams may be substituted.)

1 cup water

2 1/2 tablespoons powdered gelatin
(3 1 oz packages)

3 tablespoons sugar

1 egg (optional)

What to Do

1. Steam the **satsumaimo** for 30–40 minutes or until they are very soft. Test by piercing with a fork. Or microwave for about 10 minutes. Let cool.

2. Heat the water in a small pan. Turn off heat.

3. Sprinkle the gelatin over the water. Let stand for 3 minutes.

4. During this time, peel and mash the **satsumaimo**. Set aside.

5. Add sugar to the pan with the gelatin. Turn the heat back on low. Stir to dissolve the sugar.

6. Lightly beat the egg in a small bowl. Add to the mashed sweet potato and mix.

7. Add this to the pan with the gelatin and sugar. Mix well.

8. Pour into a mold about 7 x 7 inches. If you have a tart pan with removable bottom use that. In Japan a special mold is used.

9. Cover lightly with plastic wrap and chill in the refrigerator until firm, about 1 hour.

7. Add satsumaimo
to the gelatin

8. Pour into mold

Cut into squares

To serve, cut into 2 inch squares and arrange artistically on small plates. In Japan autumn leaves might be used to decorate each plate. Hot tea tastes great with this dessert.

Merry Ch...st

Sensei (sen-sehee) – teacher

Yuzu (yoo-zoo) – citron, a strong-flavored orange

Nenmatsu

End of the Year
December

"Hi, Sumi **Sensei**. I can't believe it's December already. Is this month special in Japan like it is back home?"

"Oh, it's special all right. In fact it is the busiest month of the year. On December 21st, the first day of winter, we put a **yuzu** (citron, a strong-flavored orange) in the bath. It's Japanese aromatherapy. December 23rd is a national holiday, Emperor Akihito's birthday. Christmas is not a day off from school or work, but it is special. Most families make or buy the official Christmas cake—a sponge cake iced with whipped cream and decorated with strawberries."

"I've never heard of cake for Christmas. We always have special cookies or bread."

"Well, after World War II, department stores in Tokyo began selling these cakes, and they really caught on."

"What about presents? Do kids get any?"

"Sure. Many families give each of their children one present from Santa on the morning of the 25th."

Nengajo (nen-gah-joh) – New Year's greeting card

Osechiryouri (oh-seh-chee-reeyōh-ree) – Japanese traditional food often prepared with a lot of salt or sugar as preservatives

Osouji (oh-sōh-jee) – major housecleaning

Toshikoshi soba (toh-shee-koh-shee soh-bah) – buckwheat noodle soup to see the old year out

"After Christmas it gets really busy. School lets out around December 28th, then everyone begins a major housecleaning called **osouji**. The work goes on for several days. Evenings are busy too because **nengajo** (New Year's greeting cards) must be addressed and mailed. Some families like to make their own design and stamp or print it on the postcards. Around December 30th, preparation of the special food for the New Year's holiday begins. Do you remember what this food is called?"

"I remember something about food in shiny boxes."

"Right. It's **osechiryouri**, and people make it at the end of the year. Plenty is made so no cooking has to be done during the first few days of the New Year."

"Do you make it too?"

"I make my favorite recipes, then I buy some of the other foods at a department store near my home. There's one special food that I make every year on December 31st. It doesn't go in a box."

"What's that?"

"It is called **toshikoshi soba** (buckwheat noodle soup). Right at midnight we Japanese like to eat a warm bowl of noodle soup to see the old year out. Outside it is so still and quiet. There's no traffic noise. Sometimes you can hear the ringing of a gong at a nearby temple. This is how we bring in the New Year."

"Will you teach me to make this special noodle soup? Then I'll make it at my house."

"It will be my pleasure, Karen."

Toshikoshi Soba   Buckwheat Noodle Soup

What You Need

4 cups water

3 tablespoons **dashi** flakes
    (or 1 packet **dashi** flakes,
    or 1 tablespoon powdered **dashi**)

5 ounces dark chicken meat

6 1/2 tablespoons soy sauce
    (You may use bottled instant soup.
    Follow instructions on the bottle.)

Noodles:
    2 quarts water
    soba noodles for 2 servings
      (or 2 packages instant ramen)

Choice of toppings:
    1 tablespoon **wakame**
    2 tablespoons fresh spinach
    1 tablespoon **nori**

What to Do

1. Bring the water to a boil. Add the **dashi**. Turn off heat and let sit for about 5 minutes.

2. Remove packet or strain the soup stock into another pan if using flakes.

3. Cut the chicken into small bite-size pieces. Add to the pan.

4. Add soy sauce and cook over low heat for 15 minutes.

5. In another pan, bring 2 quarts of water to a boil.

6. Add the noodles and cook. Follow the instructions on the package. Be sure not to overcook the noodles. Strain the noodles and rinse with cold water. Be careful, they will be hot.

Note: Some people are allergic to **soba** (buckwheat).

7. If using **wakame**, wash the salt off. Soak it in some water. Rinse again and chop. For spinach, rinse, then chop. The **nori** can be cut with scissors into very fine strips.

1. Cut chicken into pieces

To serve, place some noodles in a bowl. Ladle the soup over them. Sprinkle either **wakame**, spinach, or **nori** on top. By the way, in Japan it is OK to slurp your noodles.

6. Add the noodles to boiling water

6b. Rinse with cold water

Additional Recipes

Tara Mushiyaki   Codfish Broiled in Foil

What You Need (per person)

1 **tara** fillet (4–5 oz)
   (You may substitute other white
   fish such as tilapia, orange roughy,
   or halibut.)

aluminum foil (about 12 x 12 inches)

1 tablespoon mayonnaise

1 teaspoon soy sauce

3 snow peas

3 tablespoons **enoki** tops
   (Any mushroom can be substituted.)

What to Do

1. Make a boat

1. Fold up the sides of the aluminum foil to make a boat. Place one piece of fish in it.

2. Rinse off the snow peas and **enoki** and pat them dry. Place these on top of the fish. Spoon the soy sauce over the fish and vegetables. Plop the mayonnaise on top.

3. Fold together the sides and top of the foil boat so that no juice can leak out during cooking.

4. Place foil-wrapped fish under a broiler. Broil it about 20 minutes. Carefully open the foil wrapper. Steam will come out which will be very hot. Using a fork, gently prod the vegetables and fish. If the vegetables are tender and the fish is completely white, they're done. If the fish is still transparent in the middle, fold up the foil boat and broil a bit more.

You can also use a frying pan. Spread a little vegetable oil on the pan. Place the foil-wrapped fish in the pan. Cover and cook over low heat about 10 minutes.

Serve this along with **miso** soup and rice for a very nutritious meal.

2. Spoon soy sauce on top

3. Fold sides and top together

4. Broil

Okayu

What You Need

Version 1

1/2 cup cooked rice (per person)

2 cups warm water (per person)

1 egg

salt

Version 2

1/4 cup raw rice (per person)

1 3/4 cups water (per person)

1 egg

salt

Choice of toppings:

    1 **ume boshi**

    1 tablespoon spinach

    1 tablespoon Chinese cabbage

    1 tablespoon carrot

Rice Gruel

What to Do

Version 1

1. Put the cooked rice and water in a pan.

2. Bring to a boil. Lower heat and simmer for about 5 minutes.

3. Beat the egg in a separate bowl. Just before turning off the heat, pour it in a thin stream into the gruel. Stir very gently.

4. When the egg has cooked, turn off the heat. Add salt to taste.

Version 2

You may not have any cooked rice on hand. You'll have to start from scratch.

1. Wash the rice (see pg. 10) and put it into a deep pot. You do not let it sit this time.

2. Add water. Bring to a boil. Turn down the heat and simmer until the rice is soft (about 20 minutes). Some people like very soft rice. Others prefer it firmer. You can cook the rice as long as you like.

3. Add the egg at the end of the cooking time as described above for Version 1.

For **ume boshi okayu**, simply drop the pickled plum into the pan the last few minutes of cooking. (You eat the **ume boshi** along with the rice. It is sour but good.)

To make **okayu** with vegetables, choose several and chop into small pieces. Add them to the pan the last few minutes of cooking. (If they are cooked too long, they will lose their color and vitamins.)

1. Add the water

3. Pour in egg in a thin stream

Okayu is good when you have a stomachache.

Sumi's Sandwich House

What You Need

1 loaf of bread, not sliced

3 eggs, hardboiled

5 pieces of sandwich ham

1 cucumber, unpeeled (1 cup)

mayonnaise

salt & pepper

1/4 head of cabbage

1 package summer sausages or
    1 can Vienna sausages

What to Do

The Bread

1. Slice off 1/3 of the loaf, reserve for making extra sandwiches.

2. From the remaining bread, slice off a section 2/3's of the length.

3. Slice off the crusts. Discard. Slice this section in thirds, lengthwise. Then slice each piece in half to make 6 pieces. These pieces will become the main part of the house. Set aside.

4. Slice the crusts off the other section. Discard. Cut in half then slice each half into 1/2-inch thicknesses. These pieces will become the roof.

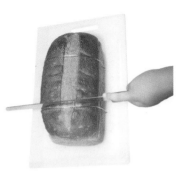

1. Slice off 1/3 loaf

2. Slice off 2/3's of
the remaining loaf

3. Slice in thirds

4. Cut in half

4b. Slice into 1/2
inch thicknesses

5. Scoop out cucumber seeds

The Filling

5. Peel the eggs and mash the yolk with a fork. Chop the whites very fine. Wash the cucumber and slice it in half lengthwise. Scoop out seeds with a small spoon. * Discard. Chop the cucumber fine and pat dry in a towel. Chop 4 slices of the ham into small pieces.

6. Mix the egg, cucumber, and ham with mayonnaise, salt, and pepper. Add just enough mayonnaise to bind the mixture together. **

7. Spread this mixture on all slices of bread, stacking them as you go. There will be thick sandwiches and thin sandwiches.

8. Cover with a towel and place a book on top to press the sandwiches down a bit. Let stand about 10 minutes.

7. Make sandwiches

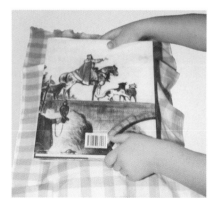

8. Press sandwiches
down with a book

11. Slice sandwiches diagonally

11b. Make the roof

13. Put sausage on as shingles

Assembly

9. Slice the cabbage thin and spread it on a large plate. This is the grass.

10. Uncover the sandwiches and separate the thick and the thin. Place the thick sandwiches on the plate. Spread a generous amount of mayonnaise on top.

11. Now slice the stack of thin sandwiches in half diagonally. Set them on top of the main section to form the roof. The tips should hang over the main section of the house a bit. Cut these sandwiches smaller if they don't fit right on top of the house.

12. Fill in any gaps with extra sandwich filling or make more sandwiches from the reserve bread in #1. Use mayonnaise as "glue" as needed. Toothpicks can be inserted to help hold the roof on the base.

13. Cut remaining piece of ham into window shapes and a door and "glue" them on. Slice the sausages into circles or log shapes and "glue" them onto the roof as shingles. You may fly a flag from the roof or add a chimney for Santa to come down. There are lots of ways to liven up the scene.

* Soggy cucumbers would make the sandwiches soggy. The seeds contain the most water so they must be removed.

** Again, to avoid soggy sandwiches, keep the mayonnaise to a minimum.

Sometimes it is hard to find bread that is not sliced. You can use firm, sliced sandwich bread. Eight slices make the base and 3 1/2 slices make the roof.

Be sure to eat this house fairly quickly. It doesn't keep well.

RECIPE	SERVINGS	TIME	DIFFICULTY
Apple Kinton	5	25 min. microwave 45 min. steam	2
Miso Soup	4-5	25 min.	2
Vinegared Rice with Colorful Toppings	5	50 min.	4
Rice Balls	4-5	10 min.	3-4
Curry and Rice	5	1 hr. 20 min.	4
Hydrangea Flower Gelatin	5	1 hr. 10 min.	3
Japanese Omelet	4	<10 min.	3
Shaved Ice	variable	5 min.	1
Boiled Vegetables	4-5	45 min.	3
Flavored Rice	5	30 min.	3
Jellied Sweet Potato	6	1 hr. 25 min. microwave 1 hr. 45 min. steam	2
Buckwheat Noodle Soup	2-4	25 min.	3
Codfish Baked in Foil	variable	30 min.	2
Rice Gruel	variable	25 min.	2
Sumi's Sandwich House	8-10	1 hr.	4

Key: 1-easy   4-more difficult

Recipes In Japanese

Recipes 日本語版

覚え書き

お買い物の目安

　すみ先生は新鮮な野菜や良質の肉、添加物のない自然食品など、健康的な食材を買うことが大切だと考えています。もし、あなたが日本固有の食材をさがすことができないときは、レシピにある代用できる食材を使ってもいいですし、もっと創造的になって、ご自分で代用できそうな食材に挑戦してみてもいいでしょう。

　お米はその国その国で違います。日本米にもっとも近いタイプはグルテンの高いお米です。これは日本米のように粘けがあります。できるならこのタイプのお米か、または中粒米を使ってください。また、同様に、お米は土地柄で料理法も変わります。例えば、日本では、調理の前にお米を何度かとぎます。でも、アメリカでは、普段お米はとぎません。実際、お米の袋には、米をとがないように注意書きがしてあります。私たちは、このお米の形を崩さないための方法を見つけました。調理の前にお米をざるに入れ、一度だけ水で流し、そのまま15～30分水を切っておくという方法です。

計量について

◆ 1カップは　200mlです。

◆ 大さじは　15mlです。

◆ 野菜は日本の標準的なサイズのものです。にんじんは太いもの、きゅうりは細いものを使っています。

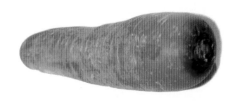 

注意すること

　まずキッチンで守る基本的な注意事項をおさらいしておきましょう。第一に、お料理を始める前には必ず手を洗うこと。鋭い刃のナイフや包丁は正しく扱うこと。火災事故をおこさないように、ガス台などで何かを調理している間は絶対にキッチンを離れてはいけません。どうしても離れなくてはならないときは、誰かに火を見ていてくれるようにたのみましょう。食べ物から湯気が出ている時は、なべが熱くなっているので手を入れてはいけません。なべを火からおろし、注意してふたを取ります。そして、湯気がだいたい消えてから、気をつけて中のお料理を取り出します。

◆　小さなお子さんがお料理をするときは、必ず最初から最後まで大人が付き添わなくては行けません。◆

レシピ　　**アップルきんとん**

Apple Kinton

よういするもの

さつまいも　2～3本（580g）

砂糖　大さじ3
りんご　中1個
レモン汁
＊塩

＊なくてもかまいません

つくりかた

1. さつまいもをゆでるか、蒸します。フォークがささるまで、十分にやわらかくします（30～40分）。電子レンジの場合は、10～15分調理します。

2. さつまいもを取り出し、すこし冷やします。指で皮をむき、皮は捨てます。

3. フォークかポテトマッシャーでさつまいもをつぶします。これは楽しいのよ。フードプロセッサーでもできますけどね。

4. 砂糖を混ぜます。

5. りんごを洗い、皮をむき、さいの目に切ります（無農薬りんごの場合は、皮を残してもいいでしょう）。変色しないように、レモン汁を数滴たらした水をはったボウルに、りんごをひたしておきます。

6. りんごの水をきり、さつまいもに加え、よく混ぜます。味をみてみましょう。甘さが足りなかったら、砂糖を足してね。塩味の好きな人はここで塩を入れて下さい。

・小皿に盛り付けましょう。素敵なデザートやおやつになります。

レシピ　**みそしる**

Miso Soup

よういするもの

水　5カップ
けずりぶし　山盛り大さじ3
　（または　だしの素パック
　　　　　　　　　　　1包み）
　（または　粉末だし　大さじ1）

野菜の組み合わせ
　（お好みの組み合わせを選んでね）

　じゃがいも　3/4カップ
　わかめ　大さじ3
　　（または　ほうれんそう）

　とうふ　1丁
　　（10cm×10cm）
　ほうれんそう　大さじ3

　大根　3/4〜1カップ
　ねぎ　1/4カップ

みそ　大さじ3

つくりかた

1. 水をなべに入れ、沸かします。けずりぶしを入れて火を止め、そのまま5分おきます。これで、だしがとれます。

2. だしの素パックを使った場合はこれを取り出します。けずりぶしは後で使えるので、別のなべにだし汁を漉しておきます。

3. じゃがいもを一口大に切ります。だしに入れて柔らかくなるまで煮ます。

4. わかめの塩抜きをします。じゃがいもをゆでている間に、わかめを水にひたしておきます。新しい水にとってもう一度さらし、一口大に切ります。それぞれのお椀に一人分ずつ入れておきます。

5. みそをだしに加えます。2本の大さじを使いましょう。1本のさじにみそを盛り、それをだしの中に半分ほどつかるくらいに入れ、もう1本のさじでみそをだしに溶き混ぜていきます。(それほど難しくはないよ)。ごく短い時間、煮立てます。

6. できあがったみそ汁を、わかめを入れておいた椀によそります。

・とうふとほうれんそうで作るときは、まず初めにとうふの水切りをします。ほうれんそうは洗って、一口大に切ります。みそは最初にだしに溶いておき、最後にほうれんそうととうふを加えて軽く煮ます（煮込みすぎると、とうふは崩れてしまいますし、ほうれんそうは色が抜けてしまいますから）。

・大根とねぎで作るときは、大根を切ってだしで煮ます。ねぎはみそを加える数分前にだしに入れて、最後にみそを溶きます。

メモ：日本のお料理ではここで「節約」をします。すみ先生は残ったけずりぶしで「二番だし」をとります。最初に使った水の半分の量の水にけずりぶしを入れ、煮立てます。それを漉して、とっておきます。この「二番だし」は他のお料理を作るときに使うことができます。

レシピ　　**ちらしずし**

Vinegared Rice with Colorful Toppings

よういするもの

米　3カップ　（といで、ざるにとっておく）
水　3と1/3カップ

合わせ酢
　酢　1/3カップ
　砂糖　大さじ2
　塩　小さじ1と1/2
　＊ごま　適量

具材（トッピング）
　しいたけ　5枚
　　しょうゆ　大さじ1
　　砂糖　大さじ1
　　＊みりん　大さじ1
　卵　2個
　にんじん・グリーンピース　（切って）3/4カップ（＊ミックスベジタブルを使ってもよいでしょう）
　かに缶　1個
　ハム　1パック（4～5枚入り）
　きゅうり　1本
　＊のり　1枚

＊お好みで入れてください

+メモ：「無洗米」を使うときは、米をざるに入れ、水でざっと流してから、おいておきます。

つくりかた

1. 大きなボウルで米をとぎます（＋）。にごった水は捨て、3～4回とぎましょう。それから米をざるにあけ、そのまま15～30分置いておきます。手でお米をとぐのは楽しいものよ！

2. 大きなおなべに米と水を入れます。

3. ふたをして、中火にかけます。煮立ったら弱火にして、水が完全になくなるまで、10～12分静かに煮ます。

4. 火を止め、ふたをしたまま5～6分おきます。

5. 大きなボウルにご飯をあけます（もし、木製のボウルがあったら、それを使いましょう）。

6. 酢、砂糖、塩をよく混ぜ、それをご飯の上にふりかけます。木製のおしゃもじでやさしく混ぜ合わせてください。この間、早くさますために、うちわで扇ぎます。ご飯から湯気が出なくなるまで扇いでください。誰かに手伝ってもらえると助かるわよ。炒ったごまを混ぜて、おいておきます。

7. 干ししいたけを使うときは、熱めのお湯で柔らかくなるまでもどします。余分な水気をきって、石づきを取り除き、細切りにします。生しいたけを使うときは、石づきを取って、細切りにします。それを小なべに入れ、全体がかぶるくらいの水を入れます。しょうゆ、砂糖、みりんを加え、弱火にかけて、5分ほど、または水分がなくなるまで煮ます。おなべから目を離さないように。水気がなくなると、しょうゆや砂糖は焦げやすいのです。しいたけを小なべから取り出し、お皿にとっておきましょう。

8. フライパンに油を薄く敷き、卵に小さじ1の砂糖を入れ、炒り卵を作ります。あるいは、薄焼き卵を作り、それを細切りにしたものを使ってもいいですね。

9. にんじんを5円玉の形や、星型で抜きます。塩少々を加えた水でゆでて、ざるにあけ、水気をきってからご飯に混ぜます。グリーンピースは塩ゆでします。（ミックスベジタブルを使うときは、冷凍のままざるに入れ、流水で解凍します。ペーパータオルで水気をとりましょう）。

10. かに缶の水気をきっておきます。

11. ハムを細切りにします。きゅうりは、水洗いしてから細長く切り、それを三等分の長さに切ります。

12. 卵とハムを半分残して、あとの具材はご飯にかるく混ぜ込んでください。

13. 残しておいた卵とハム、細切りにしたのりを、混ぜごはんの上から散らします。

レシピ   **おむすび**   Rice Balls

よういするもの   つくりかた

米 1と1/2カップ   **1.** 68ページの作り方にしたがって、米をた   **6.**外側にのりを巻いてもいいでしょう。
水 1と3/4カップ   いておきます。   作っているときに巻いてもいいし、ラ
水を入れた小さなボウル   ップで包んでおいて食べるときに巻い
塩 小さじ1   **2.** にぎりやすくなるまで冷ましましょう。   てもいいですよ。

中に入れる具のヴァリエーション: **3.** 水を入れた小さなボウルに塩を入れます。
  ツナ缶（水気を切っておく）   軽い塩味がつくくらいにね。
  ハム（食べやすい大きさに切って）
  調理した鶏肉（同上）   **4.** 指を塩水にひたして、ご飯を5〜6個のボ
  ほぐした鮭   ールに分けておきます。

のり   **5.** 手についたご飯はボウルの水に入れて、
                                         はらいます。さあ、握りましょう。分けたボ
                                         ールのひとつを手に取り、反対の手で固
                                         く押し付けます。ボールをひっくりかえして、
                                         同じように握ります。ひっくりかえして握る、
                                         ひっくりかえして握る・・・この繰り返しです。
                                         （ご飯が指にくっつきだしたら、途中で塩
                                         水で払い落としてください）。雪球を作る
                                         のに似ているでしょう？ゴールはおむす
                                         びのご飯がしっかりくっつくまで。でも、投
                                         げつけても壊れないほど固くしないように
                                         ね。「簡単ではないけれど、**がんばって
                                         ね！**」（すみ先生はそう言います。）

                                         　握っている途中で、ツナやハムなど
                                         好きな具を真ん中に入れることができ
                                         ます。すみ先生のおすすめはツナです。

レシピ　**カレーライス**

Curry and Rice

よういするもの

米　3カップ
水　3と1/3カップ

カレーソース
　牛乳　2/3カップ
　カレー粉　小さじ2と1/2～小さじ3
　小麦粉　大さじ3

＊（インスタントカレーの素を使うこともできます。そのときは、パッケージの作り方にしたがってください）

牛肉または鶏肉　450g
　塩・コショー
じゃがいも　3個
にんじん　1本
玉ねぎ　1個
りんご　中1個
植物油　大さじ2
水　1と1/2カップ
コンソメ（固形）　1と1/2個
塩　小さじ1

つくりかた

1. 68ページの作り方にしたがって、米をたいておきます。

2. カレーソースを作りましょう。小さななべに牛乳を入れ、弱火にかけます。かきまぜながら、カレー粉と小麦粉を少しずつ加えます。とろみがついたら火からおろし、おいておきます。

3. 肉を大きめの一口大に切ります。

4. にんじんの皮をむき、一口大に切ります。

5. じゃがいもの皮をむき、大きめの一口大にきります。変色しないように、水をはったボウルにつけておきましょう。

6. 玉ねぎの皮をむき、ほかの野菜と同じ大きさに切ります。

7. 重くてしっかりしたなべを用意します。油をしいて、肉と野菜を入れ、肉の表面が茶色になり、玉ねぎが柔らかくなるまで炒めます（じゃがいもはおなべに入れる前にしっかり水気を切っておくこと）。塩・コショー少々をふります。

8. ここでコンソメ・塩・水を加えて、よく混ぜます。

9. ふたをして中火にし、肉が十分煮えるまで、約10分煮込みます。

10. カレーソースを加えます。少しずつ入れて、その度によくかきまぜましょう。

11. りんごの皮をむき、すりおろしてなべに加えます。よくかきまぜます。

12. ふたをして、よーく風味が出るまで弱火で約40分煮込みましょう。なべ底にカレーがくっつかないように、ときどきかきまぜてください。味をみて、たりないようだったら塩を足してください。

レシピ　**あじさいかん**

Hydrangea Flower Gelatin

よういするもの

水　2と1/2カップ
粉ゼラチン　大さじ2と1/2
砂糖　大さじ4
濃縮グレープジュース　大さじ2
　（冷凍のでもいいです）
ペパーミントエッセンス　小さじ1/4
牛乳　大さじ5

あじさいの葉　数枚
　（別の植物の葉でもよい。
庭を消毒した後の葉は使わないで下さい。
危ないですから。）

つくりかた

1. 小なべで水を温め、火を止めます。

2. 粉ゼラチンを1に振りいれ、3分間おいておきます。

3. 小なべを再び弱火にかけ、砂糖を加えて溶けるまでかきまぜます。

4. 溶けたゼラチン液を4個の容器に分け入れます。容器は、あれば底の平らなものにしてください。4個の容器にそれぞれ均等になるように入れてみましょう。

5. ひとつめの容器にグレープジュースを加えてまぜます。

6. ふたつめの容器にはペパーミントエッセンスを加えてまぜます。

7. みっつめの容器には牛乳を加えてまぜます。

8. みっつの容器にふたをします。ないときはラップをかけて。冷蔵庫に入れてゼラチンが固まるまで、約1時間冷やします。

9. 何も加えていない残りの容器は、30分待ってから、ふたをして冷蔵庫に約30分入れ、やわらかめに固めます。

10. 飾り付け用に直径15センチのガラスのボウルの内側を水で濡らしておきます。

11. 味付けをしたゼラチンの容器を冷蔵庫から出し、いろいろな形に切ります。サイコロ型や星型、丸型など・・・。ひとつひとつの大きさはだいたい7ミリ〜1センチ。それから、飾りつけのボウルにそっと入れましょう。色とりどりに混ぜてごらんなさい。

　・　もし、ゼラチンが容器にくっついて取れないときは、容器の底を熱湯を入れたなべに15秒ほどつけます。そうすると、底のゼラチンが溶けて、するりと出てきますよ）。

12. あじさいの葉を洗い、ゼラチンのまわり
に差し込みます。葉っぱの先はボウル
のふちから少し出るようにしましょう。そ
うすると、ほら、大きなあじさいのように
見えるでしょう？

13. 味付けをしていないゼラチンを冷蔵庫
から出します。このゼラチンはやわらか
めですが、流れてしまうほどやわらかく
てはいけません。スプーンで味付けを
したゼラチンの上からとろりとかけましょ
う。これで、このあじさいにきれいなつや
ができるでしょう。もう一度冷蔵庫に入
れ、15分ほど冷やし固めます。

・テーブルの真ん中にボウルを出し、そ
れぞれの小さなボウルにスプーンで取
り分けます。素敵なデザートやおやつ
になります。お茶とクッキーと一緒でも
いいですし、もちろんそのままでも。

レシピ **薄焼き卵**

Japanese Omelet

よういするもの

つくりかた

直径15センチのフライパン
植物油
卵 3個
砂糖 小さじ2
しょうゆ 小さじ1

マヨネーズ
薄切りにしたきゅうり

1. 小さなボウルに卵と砂糖としょうゆを入れ、よく混ぜ合わせます。

2. フライパンに植物油をしきます(油がたまるようでは多すぎます。ペーパータオルでそっとふきとりましょう)。

3. フライパンを弱火にかけます。

4. 卵液の1/3を注ぎ入れます。フライパンを持ち上げ、軽くゆすりながら均一になるように広げましょう。弱火のまま、卵が固まるまで1分ほど待ちます。フライパンを火からおろします。

5. へらを使って、フライパンの向こう側から自分のほうに薄焼き卵を巻きこんできます。

6. 巻いた薄焼き卵をフライパンからまな板に移し、広げます。

7. フライパンに油を足し、ペーパータオルで薄くのばします。

8. もう一度フライパンを火にかけ、残りの卵液の半量を流し入れます。

9. 一回目と同じように焼いて、最初の薄焼き卵の上にのせます。

10. 最後に残った卵液を同じように焼いて、重ねます。(上手になってくると、これよりも少しの卵液を何回も入れることで、もっとずっと薄い薄焼き卵が作れるようになりますよ。がんばってください)。

11. 重ねた薄焼き卵をしっかりと巻きます。端から4センチの長さに切ります。

・両端を切り落として、小さなお皿に並べます。マヨネーズ少量をスプーンで上からたらします。延ばさないように。マヨネーズの上に薄切りにしたきゅうりをかざりましょう。

レシピ　**かきごおり**

Shaved Ice

よういするもの

かき氷器　または　フードプロセッサー
氷　2カップ（一人分）
フルーツシロップ　大さじ3
　（お好みの味を選んでね）
　　・いちご
　　・ブルーベリー
　　・ラズベリー
　　・メロン
　　・グレープ
　など

つくりかた

1. 氷をかき氷器かフードプロセッサーに入
れます。

2. 食べやすいかき氷にしましょう。

3. かき氷をボウルか大きめのカップに入れ
ます。

4. シロップを上からかけます。

レシピ　**煮物**

Boiled Vegetables

よういするもの

しいたけ　3枚
にんじん　1本
さといも　中3個　（または　じゃがいも　2個）
さやえんどう　10〜12個
鴨肉　110g
竹の子　大さじ3　（または　栗の水煮）

※二番だし　1と1/2カップ（67ページ参照）
砂糖　大さじ1
しょうゆ　大さじ2
料理酒　大さじ2
＊みりん　大さじ2
＊味の素　ひとつまみ

※普通のだしでもよいです
＊なくてもかまいません

つくりかた

1. 乾燥しいたけを使うときは、熱湯で柔らかくなるまでもどします。

2. にんじんの皮をむき、大きめの一口大に切っておきます。

3. さといもを洗い、皮をむきます。すべりやすいので気をつけてね。冷水にひたしておきましょう。

4. さやえんどうを洗い、へたとすじを取っておきます。

5. 鴨肉を小さめの一口大に切ります。

6. 生の竹の子を使うときは洗って水気をきり、一口大にスライスします。缶詰の場合は水気をきっておきます。

7. しいたけとさといもの水気をきります。しいたけをもどした水はとっておきましょう。しいたけの石づきを切り、捨てます。さといもはそのまま使いますが、大きい場合は半分に切りましょう。

8. さやえんどう以外の全部の野菜と鴨肉をなべに入れ、二番だし、砂糖、しょうゆ、酒を加えます。しいたけをもどした水も入れます。ふたをして強火にかけ、煮立ったら弱火にします。野菜が柔らかくなるまで12分ほど煮込みます。

9. みりんとさやえんどうを加えます。最後の数分はふたを取って煮ます。風味をつけるために味の素を入れ、よくかきまぜます。

レシピ　**あじごはん**

Flavored Rice

よういするもの

米　3カップ
だし汁　3と1/2カップ（作り方　9. を見て）

鶏ムネ肉　1枚（185g）
しょうゆ　大さじ1と1/2
料理酒　大さじ1と1/2
砂糖　大さじ1

にんじん　1/3本
＊ごぼう　12センチ
えのきだけ　（先のほうだけ）大さじ3
竹の子　大さじ3
しょうゆ　大さじ1

パセリ　大さじ2

＊なくてもよいです

つくりかた

1. 68ページの作り方にしたがって、米をとぎます。

2. 鶏肉を小さめに切ります。

3. なべに鶏肉を入れ、全体がかぶるくらいに水を入れます。しょうゆ、酒、砂糖を加えます。

4. 鶏肉に火がとおるまで煮ます。

5. 鶏肉を取り出します。煮汁はとっておきましょう。

6. にんじんの皮をむき、1センチほどの長さの薄切りにします。

7. 包丁の背で、ごぼうの皮をこそげます。なるべく薄く切ってください。茶色に変色しないように、水をはったボウルにひたしておきます（ごぼうは酸化するのがとても速いのです）。

8. 生の竹の子を使うときは、洗って水気をきります。缶詰の場合は水気をきっておきます。一口大に切ります。

9. パセリ以外のすべての材料を深いなべに入れます。鶏肉をゆでた煮汁に水を加えて、全体で2と1／2カップになるようにします。それをなべに入れ、しょうゆ大さじ1、塩ひとつまみを加えます。

10. 米が噴き出さないように気をつけながら、約12分弱火で炊き上げます。

11. 火を止めて15分むらします。おしゃもじでやさしく混ぜ合わせ、みじん切りにしたパセリを混ぜ入れます。

・お弁当にもうってつけです。あたたかいご飯は卵スープと一緒に。デザートにはオレンジのスライスがよく合いますよ。

レシピ　**さつまいもようかん**

Jellied Sweet Potato

よういするもの

さつまいも　2本（500g）

水　1カップ
寒天　1本
　または　粉ゼラチン
　　　　　大さじ2と1/2
砂糖　大さじ3
＊卵　1個

＊なくてもかまいません

つくりかた

1. さつまいもを蒸すかゆでます。フォークで楽に刺せるぐらいに柔らかくします（30〜40分）。電子レンジの場合は、10〜15分調理します。そのまま冷ましておきます。

2. 水を小なべに入れ沸騰させて、火を止めます。

3. 寒天を小なべに入れます。粉ゼラチンの場合は、小なべに振り入れ、3分間おきます。

4. この間に、さつまいもの皮をむき、つぶして、おいておきます。

5. 3の小なべに砂糖を加えます。小なべを弱火にかけます。かきまぜて、砂糖が溶けたら火を止めます。

6. 小さなボウルに卵をときます。さつまいもに加えて、よく混ぜ合わせます。

7. 5の小なべにさつまいもを入れ、よく混ぜ合わせます。

8. 16cmx17cm型に流しいれます。もし、底が取れる寒天型をお持ちでしたら、それを使ってください。

9. 型に軽くラップをかけて、冷蔵庫に入れ、固まるまで約1時間冷やします。

・5センチ角に切り分けて、小皿に並べましょう。もちろん、芸術的にアレンジしたっていいのよ。熱いお茶がそれはそれはよく合います。

レシピ　**年越しそば**

Buckwheat Noodle Soup

よういするもの

つくりかた

水　5カップ
けずりぶし　大さじ3
　（または　だしの素パック　1包み）
　（または　粉末だしの素　大さじ1）

鴨肉　150g
しょうゆ　大さじ6と1／2
　（瓶入りのつゆを使ってもかまいませ
ん。そのときは瓶の説明に従ってください）

そば　2人分
　（または　インスタントラーメン　2パック）

メモ：ときどきそばでアレルギー症状を起こ
す人がいます。

薬味のヴァリエーション
　わかめ　大さじ1
　生のほうれんそう　大さじ2
　のり　大さじ1

1. 水をなべに入れ、沸騰させてだしを加えます。火を止めて、そのまま5分間おいておきます。

2. だしパックのときは取り出します。けずりぶしを使うときは別のなべにだし汁を漉しましょう。

3. 鶏肉を小さめに切り、だし汁のなべに加えます。

4. しょうゆを加え、弱火で15分間煮ます。

5. 別のなべに水2リットルを沸かします。

6. そばを袋の説明に従ってゆでます。くれぐれも、ゆですぎないように。

7. そばをざるにあげ、流水にさらします。熱くなっているので、気をつけてね。

8. わかめを薬味に使うときは、塩を洗い流します。水に5分ほどつけておきましょう。もう一度洗い、余分な水気を絞ります。それから、細かく刻みます。ほうれんそうの場合は、洗って切ります。のりははさみを使って細長く切りましょう。いずれも別のお皿にとっておきます。

・そばはボウルに盛り、鶏肉入りつゆを上からおたまでかけます。わかめ、ほうれんそう、のりなどを上に散らします。

レシピ　　**たらの蒸し焼き**

Codfish Broiled in Foil

よういするもの

（1人前）

＊**たらの切り身 （約120g）**
クッキングホイル（30センチ×30センチ）
マヨネーズ　大さじ1
しょうゆ　小さじ1と1/2

さやえんどう　3枚
えのきだけ （先だけを）大さじ3
（他のきのこでもかまいません）

＊**たらの代わりに、おひょうなどの白身魚を使ってもいいですよ。**

つくりかた

1. クッキングホイルを船のような形に折ります。その中にたらを置きます。

2. さやえんどうとえのきだけを洗い、ペーパータオルの上に広げて水気を取ります。それから、たらの上に並べます。たらと野菜の上から、しょうゆをスプーンでかけます。マヨネーズをてっぺんにぽとりと落とします。

3. 調理中に汁がもれないように、クッキングホイルの端とてっぺんを合わせて折ります。

4. ホイル包みのたらを肉焼き機の下に入れます。約20分焼いてください（肉焼き機がないときは、フライパンでもできます。油を薄くしたフライパンにホイル包みを置き、弱火で5〜7分蒸し焼きにします）。ホイルを開くときは気をつけて。とても熱い湯気がでてきますから。フォークでたらと野菜をそっと刺してみましょう。野菜がすっかり柔らかくなり、たらが白くなっていればできあがりです。たらの真ん中がまだ透き通っているようでしたら、もう一度ホイルを包みなおして、もう少し焼きましょう。

・みそ汁とごはんで、栄養満点の食事になりますよ。

レシピ　**おかゆ**

Rice Gruel

よういするもの

「つくりかた」その１の場合
　ごはん　1／2カップ（1人前）
　湯　2カップ（1人前）

「つくりかた」その２の場合
　米　1／4カップ（1人前）
　水　1と3／4カップ（1人前）

お好みの具

　卵　1個
　うめぼし　1個
　ほうれんそう　大さじ1
　白菜　大さじ1
　にんじん　大さじ1

つくりかた　その１

1. ごはんとお湯をなべに入れます。

2. 火にかけて煮立ったら弱火にし、5分ほど煮ます。

3. ボウルに卵を溶き、火を止める直前におかゆの中に細く流し入れます。しずかにかきまぜます。

4. 卵が煮えたら火を止め、塩で味をつけます。

つくりかた　その２

ごはんがないときはお米から作りましょう。

1. 68ページのつくり方に従って、米をとぎ、深鍋に入れます。今回は水にひたしておく必要はありません。

2. 水を加え、火にかけます。沸騰したら火を弱め、米が柔らかくなるまで約20分煮込みます。ご自分の好きな柔らかさにしていいのですよ。とても柔らかいのが好きな人もいますし、もう少し固めがいい、というひともいますから。

3. 「つくりかた　その１」の最後に挙げた材料を、火を止める数分前に加えて煮ます。

・梅干がゆは、火を止める数分前にうめぼしを落とすだけです。

・野菜がゆを作るときは、好きな野菜をいくつか組み合わせ、細かく刻みます。火を止める数分前になべに入れて、煮ます（あんまり長く煮込まないこと。色もビタミンも失われてしまいますからね）。

レシピ　**すみ先生のサンドイッチハウス**　　　　# Sumi's Sandwich House

よういするもの

食パン　1本（スライスしていないもの）
固ゆで卵　3個
サンドイッチ用ハム　4～5枚
きゅうり　2本
マヨネーズ
塩・コショー

きゃべつ　1/4個
小さめのソーセージ　1袋（ゆでておく）

つくりかた

1. 食パンの1/3を切り落とします。これは使わないので、別のときにサンドイッチを作るのにとっておいてください。

2. 残ったパンを横長に置いて、2/3の長さに切ります。

3. みみを落とします。今度は横長にみっつに切り分けます。このみっつは半分に切って。全部で6枚になります。これがおうちの土台になります。

4. 2で切り取った残りの1/3のほうのパンもみみを落とします。こちらは半分に切ったあと、厚さ1.5センチにスライスします。これはおうちの屋根になります。

5. 卵のからをむいて、黄身をつぶします。白身はみじんぎりにします。きゅうりの皮をむき、半分の長さに切ります。種を取り除きます＊。きゅうりをみじんぎりにし、ペーパータオルの上で水気を取ります。ハム4枚は粗みじんに切ります。

6. 卵、きゅうり、ハムをマヨネーズと塩・コショーであえます＊＊。マヨネーズは全体が隠れるくらいの量を入れてください。

7. 6をスライスしたパン全部にぬってください。厚いサンドイッチと薄いサンドイッチにタオルをかけ、てっぺんに 本を載せて重しにします。こうして10分ほ どおいておきます。

8. きゃべつを千切りにして、大皿に敷きます。こうすると草のようになるでしょう？

9. タオルと本を取り、厚いサンドイッチと薄いサンドイッチに分けます。厚いほうを大皿に置きます。これでおうちの土台ができました。てっぺんにマヨネーズをたっぷり塗ってください。

10. 薄いほうのサンドイッチは斜め半分に切ります。これを土台のサンドイッチの上に屋根になるように置きましょう。先が土台から少し出るように。もし、大きすぎてしまったら、おうちにぴったり合うように少し小さく切ってください。

11. 残ったサンドイッチフィリングで壁の隙間をうめていきます。**1**で残しておいたパンで別にサンドイッチを作ってもいいですね。必要ならマヨネーズを「接着剤」に使ってください。屋根に楊枝をさすと、しっかりしますよ。

12. 残りのハムを窓とドアの形に切り、マヨネーズの接着剤でおうちに貼り付けます。ソーセージを丸型や丸太型に切り、屋根に貼り付けます。旗が上がっているようにもできるし、サンタ・クロースがきてくれるように煙突をつくることもできますよ。

　みなさんが住みたいおうちになるように、このサンドイッチハウスを作りましょう。
＋でも、このおうちは早めに食べましょう。あんまり長くはもたないから。

＊水っぽいきゅうりはサンドイッチをびしょびしょにしてしまいます。種には多くの水分が含まれているので、これを取り除くのです。

＊＊ここでは、サンドイッチをびしょびしょにしないために、できるだけマヨネーズは少なく使いましょう。

Glossary of Japanese Words and Phrases

Guide to pronunciation

a – ah, as in father

e – eh, as in ten

i – ee, as in ink

o – oh, as in home

u – oo, as in too

ai – ahee, as in ice

ei – ehee, as in eight

ou – ōh, held longer as in: I want to go home!

Aikido (ahee-kee-doh) – a Japanese martial art

Ajigohan (ah-jee-goh-han) – flavored rice

Ajinomoto (ah-jee-noh-moh-toh) – monosodium glutamate (MSG), a type of salt used for bringing out the flavor of foods. It is not used in all-natural cooking.

Ajisai (ah-jee-sahee) – hydrangea flower

Ajisaikan (ah-jee-sahee-kan) – hydrangea flower gelatin

Akemashite omedetou gozaimasu (ah-keh-mah-shee-teh oh-meh-deh-tōh goh-zahee-mah-soo) – Happy New Year.

Chirashizushi (chee-rah-shee-zoo-shee) – vinegared rice with colorful toppings

Chirasu (chee-rah-soo) – sprinkle

Daikon (dahee-kon) – Japanese radish

Dashi (dah-shee) – soup stock made from dried fish. It is sold as loose flakes or shavings, in packets like tea bags, or as a powder.

Douzo ohairi kudasai (dōh-zoh oh-hahee-ree koo-dah-sahee) – Please come in.

Enoki (eh-noh-kee) – nettle mushroom

Fuku wa uchi! Oni wa soto! (foo-koo wah oo-chee oh-nee wah soh-toh) – Blessings come into the house and the devil get out!

Gambate ne! (gam-bah-teh neh) – Hang in there!

Gobo (goh-boh) – burdock root

Gochisousamadeshita (goh-chee-sōh-sah-mah-deh-shee-tah) – I have enjoyed this food (or drink) very much.

Hinadan (hee-nah-dan) – Girl's Day decoration consisting of seven steps with miniature pieces representing a royal court

Hanami (hah-nah-mee) – flower viewing

Hina Matsuri (hee-nah mah-tsoo-ree) – Girl's Day

Imohori (ee-moh-hoh-ree) – sweet potato digging

Itadakimasu (ee-tah-dah-kee-mah-soo) – I take this to eat (or drink).

Juku (joo-koo) – cram school

Kakigouri (kah-kee-gōh-ree) – shaved ice with flavored syrup

Kanji (kan-jee) – Chinese characters

Kendo (ken-doh) – Japanese fencing

Kinton (keen-ton) – sweet dish made with sweet potatoes and boiled chestnuts or apples

Kodomo no Hi (koh-doh-moh noh hee) – Children's Day

Koinobori (kohee-noh-boh-ree) – carp streamer

Mamemaki (mah-meh-mah-kee) – bean throwing ceremony

Mirin (mee-reen) – sweetened Japanese rice wine, used only for cooking

Miso (mee-soh) – fermented soy bean paste

Miso shiru (mee-soh shee-roo) – soup made with miso

Natsuyasumi (nah-tsoo-yah-soo-mee) – summer vacation

Negi (neh-gee) – long onion

Nengajo (nen-gah-joh) – New Year's greeting card

Nenmatsu (nen-mah-tsoo) – end of the year

Niban dashi (nee-ban dah-shee) – second broth, made from once-boiled dried fish used for **dashi**

Nimono (nee-moh-noh) – boiled vegetables

Nori (noh-ree) – laver, a seaweed that is pressed into sheets and dried

Obento (oh-ben-toh) – Japanese box lunch

Ohimesama (oh-hee-meh-sah-mah) – princess

Okayu (oh-kah-yoo) – rice gruel

Omusubi (oh-moo-soo-bee) – rice balls. Also called **onigiri**.

Origami (oh-ree-gah-mee) – folded paper figures

Orihime (oh-ree-hee-meh) – Weaver or Vega star

Osechiryouri (oh-seh-chee-reeyōh-ree) – Japanese traditional food often prepared with a lot of salt or sugar as preservatives

Oshougatsu (oh-shōh-gah-tsoo) – New Year's Day

Osouji (oh-sōh-jee) – major housecleaning

Otoshidama (oh-toh-shee-dah-mah) – money given to children at New Year's

Otsukimikai (oh-tsoo-kee-mee-kahee) – Harvest Moon Celebration

Ouji (ōh-jee) – prince

Roujin no Hi (rōh-jeen noh hee) – Respect for the Elderly Day

Sake (sah-keh) – rice wine

Sakura (sah-koo-rah) – cherry tree or blossom

Samurai (sah-moo-rahee) – a Japanese warrior

Satoimo (sah-toh-ee-moh) – taro, plant similar to a potato

Satsumaimo (sah-tsoo-mahee-moh) – Japanese sweet potato

Satsumaimo youkan (sah-tsoo-mahee-moh yōh-kan) – jellied sweet potato

Sensei (sen-sehee) – teacher

Setsubun (seh-tsoo-boon) – roughly translated: Spring is just around the corner.

Shiitake (shee ee-tah-keh) – large flat mushroom

Shuubun (shoo-boon) – day and night are equal but days will start to get shorter

Soba (soh-bah) – buckwheat or buckwheat noodles

Susuki (soo-soo-kee) – Japanese pampas grass

Tai'iku no Hi (tahee-koo noh hee) – Field Day

Takenoko (tah-keh-noh-koh) – bamboo shoot

Tanabata (tah-nah-bah-tah) – Festival of the Weaver's Star

Tara (tah-rah) – codfish

Tara mushiyaki (tah-rah moo-shee-yah-kee) – codfish baked in foil

Tofu (toh-foo) – soybean curd

Toshikoshi soba (toh-shee-koh-shee soh-bah) – buckwheat noodle soup to see the old year out

Tsuyu (tsoo-yoo) – the rainy season

Ume boshi (oo-meh boh-shee) – pickled plum

Undokai (oon-doh-kahee) – athletic meet

Ushiboshi (oo-shee-boh-shee) – Cowherd or Altair star

Usuyakitamago (oo-soo-yah-kee-tah-mah-goh) – thin rolled omelet

Wakame (wah-kah-meh) – variety of seaweed, usually dried or partially dried

Yuzu (yoo-zoo) – citron, a strong-flavored orange

Other words to know

Doumo arigatou gozaimasu (dōh-moh ah-ree-gah-tōh goh-zahee-mah-soo) – thank you very much

Kon'nichi wa (kon-nee-chee wah) – hello

Sayounara (sah-yōh-nah-rah) – good-bye

Afterword to Parents and Teachers

Introducing children to dishes prepared with natural foods helps insure their permanent place in the diet. As educators at the most basic level, we who pass on our traditions of eating and cooking leave an indelible legacy for the next generation. In much the same way, an appreciation of beauty is acquired through the sharing of beautiful images with our children. We hope you have found satisfaction in both areas.

Contributors

Sumiko Nagasawa taught cooking for fifty years to a wide variety of students. Sumi **Sensei** taught girls and boys basic Japanese cooking at elementary schools. Most of her students, however, were homemakers or women getting ready to set up housekeeping. She taught Japanese cooking as well as French, South American and Chinese recipes. She held her classes in cooking studios, in her own home, and in students' homes. Her study of cooking has taken her to places like Lyon, France; Rio de Janeiro and São Paulo, Brazil; as well as Mexico. Her favorite recipe is **ajigohan**.

Kimberly Ono lived in Japan from 1984 to 2001. She learned Japanese cooking from Sumi **Sensei** as well as from neighbors. Now she enjoys preparing Japanese food for her family and friends in New Jersey. She has written stories and skits for English students in Japan. Her favorite recipe is **miso shiru**.

Masami Shiga began drawing as a child. Now she paints in several styles including oil, watercolor, tole and **Nihonga** (a painting style unique to Japan). She belongs to the Hachiman group of **Nihonga** painters. Her favorite recipe is **ajisaikan**.

Miho Sakai Moyer specializes in cartoon art. She helped create the Disney character PB&J Otter and the dog in "Brand Spanking New Doug." She worked on the National Geographic Show "Spin" and did art for the *Beginner's Bible*. Miho grew up in Japan and came to the USA to train in art. She does freelance art and teaches animation. Her favorite recipe is **apple kinton**.

Doug Wille began taking pictures around 20 years ago. Now he has his own photography business, "Cheapshots," in Bridgewater, New Jersey. He likes to work in both color and black and white. His favorite recipe is **ajigohan**.

Maria Wako began writing Japanese **haiku**, poetry, and stories when she was eleven years old. She published *Hidamari no Wolfy* in 2002. Her **haiku** have been published in anthologies, collections, and magazines. Currently she is a member of the **haiku** publishing group "TOONE." Her favorite recipe is **nimono**.

Amy Tomaro is an elementary student. She likes challenging new things so she tried hand modeling for this cookbook. She found out it takes a lot of patience to pose for photographs, but she enjoyed doing it. Her favorite recipe is **usuyakitamago**.

Bob Ono is a high school student. He prefers sports but was willing to help out with this cookbook. He taste-tested all the recipes (so many times), did troubleshooting on the computer and posed for the chopstick photo. His favorite recipe is **satsumaimo youkan**.